Here's To

101 Songs and Poems about Pubs, Including in the Mornings, Afternoons, Outside, Ponderings, Evenings, Jokers, Cheers

Books by Matt Kavan

Flopping on the Deck
The Forest That Knows
Thirsty Dreams
Here For a Moment
Here's To
The Morning Catch

Here's To

101 Songs and Poems about Pubs, Including in
the Mornings, Afternoons, Outside, Ponderings,
Evenings, Jokers, Cheers

Matt Kavan

Matt Kavan
2014

First Printing: 2014

ISBN: 978-1-312-36891-0

Matt Kavan
www.mattkavan.com

Book Cover Graphics: The paintings were created by Paul Kavan.

Ordering Information:
Special discounts are available on quantity purchases by corporations, associations, educators, and others. For details, contact the publisher at the above listed address.

Dedication

To the pubs of old
Where stories are told
Can play a few notes
Say a few jokes

Light up a smoke
Without any ropes
Some call it gold
A home from the road

Escape from the lore
Opening a door
Cheers for before
And at least one more

Contents

Introduction

Hitting the pub or having a few can be lots of things to different people, it's what people do when they're not working, not at home, and not busy with another activity but simply hanging out, relaxing, or having a few conversations. While sports games or TVs may be occasionally blasting away, usually they're not and you're resorted to talking with others, watching the general activities of whatever's happening, or on your own and reading a paper, book, or other activity.

When traveling, it's often the first thing one will do after arriving and settling in, hit a pub to get things sorted out. When done working, it can be a place for colleagues to get out in a non-office atmosphere, and in the process venting on some of the real problems or even a few solutions. When working from home, hitting the pub can be an escape, getting out and having a few conversations with others in the community. If a musician, it can be going to hear others or even sharing some of your own tunes.

While there you can meet up with old friends or meet a few new ones, all with the common purpose of unwinding and taking a break. Depending on the pub, you can try different beers from all sorts of places, using recipes or general ingredients going back thousands of years. Mythology is filled with tales of drunken festivities, using beverages as a bridge to new ideas or activities, leaving the coward at the door. Of course, like anything it can occasionally go too far, hangovers, saying things that could be misunderstood, and other accidents but those are the exceptions and if done with the sole purpose of unwinding or finding the fool or joker, no worries. It's only when you're no longer unwinding, getting all serious again that problems begin to surface. Sort of what you could say is the opposite of what most people do for work, which maybe is sort of the point, getting balanced out again.

Here's To is 101 songs and poems about hitting the pub or really just taking a break for a bit. They're organized in seven sections including Mornings for either very late nights or recoveries, Afternoons for when calling it an early day, taking a break, or just happen to be in the neighborhood, Outside for when having a few and not in the normal indoor environment, Ponderings for many of the random thoughts one gets after a few, Evenings for as things start to pick up including the music, Jokers for the fools and clowns entering the picture, and finally Cheers for what you could call some drinking or celebration songs. Which is what I'd say is how most days should end if reality didn't get in the way.

Mornings

A Sponge

I'm all dried out
Hangover moved in
Dreaming of water
Jumping all in
No amount is enough
I need an ocean
A river to flow
I am receiving
Such is the curse
When waking up again
A bought or drought
A sponge I am

Coffee

Coffee in the morning
Start with a spark
Wake from the dreary
Lighten the dark

Coffee in the afternoon
A little extra pickup
Just a few more hours
Call it a rest stop

Coffee in the evening
After food and some drink
With the moon and stars
A little sprint before sleep

So much coffee
Some say too much
Not getting drunk
But still a crutch

No arguments there
But it feels like a treat
With fresh ground beans
And water with heat

When it's cold outside
Maybe snow on the ground
You need to stay warm
No running around

I've tried plenty of teas
Much better when warmer
I'm sure you'd agree
Coffee when colder

Dawn to Noon

As the sun is rising
I'll celebrate the new
Everyday a rain
With the morning dew
Enjoy it while it lasts
The sun soon to burn
Mistakes of the past
Getting ready for high noon

Happy Hour Mornings

Working so late, sometimes until dawn
Where can one go, for a happy hour song
To meet a few others, that are in the same boat
Raise a glass with the sun, taking off the coat
With few and far between, you make your own scene
Grab your own six pack, find a meadow or beach
Hanging with the birds, the first of the day
Cheers to the ones, that join up to play

In the Morning

In the morning is only
A cup of coffee
Maybe an Irish
Or Bloody Mary
Either way
Start up the day
Opening doors
Mind to wake

Quixote Morning

When the sun is rising
Coffee I'll have
Until hours later
A christening is had
For what the hell
Life is too short
Ringing a bell
Finding the worth
Of where it goes
One step at a time
Letting it flow
And all will be fine

When All is Silent

It's six am, most call it a morning
For others it's the end of an evening
Both are changing, riding the edge
Coffee or drinking, no words are said
Plans wrapping up or starting anew
Whatever is done, letting it loose
Seeing the sun, the blink of a moment
Nobody has won, when all is silent

Where is My Cup of Coffee

Where is my cup of coffee
That I need when I wake up
Until I find not so cheery
Nothing personal, fill the cup
Or whenever tired and weary
In a fog, bleak or blurry
The caffeine climbs, straight to the mind
Where is my cup of coffee

Afternoons

Afternoon Delirium

It's sunny outside, but I'm feeling blue
The temperature rising, my nose running too
I should be in bed, but I gotta get out
Errands to run, bills to douse

Coughing up a lung, I struggle along
Walking a mile, hear the ravens song
Hitting the bank, a withdrawal for the trouble
Maybe just one, beer from the pub

Just right for a fever, hot and cold spells
Throw in a shot, a party in hell
It's only one pm, but the bar is filling up
All sorts of characters, emptying their cup

Someone buys an elder, in the corner a drink
He say you'll regret it, I'm not what you think
With sun going down, why not, you asked it
Another twist of the tail, he starts to blather

For the next two hours, he went into detail
Of all his enemies, what's wrong with cultures
In a shiny new suit, his gut bulging out
Looking down his glasses, blabber and shout

It didn't take long, people grabbed another ride
No longer listening, all the people he fired
Sitting back down, finishing my beer
Hearing the tunes, another's helper cheer

8

An Afternoon Evening

Hitting the pub, while doing errands
At the local market street
Just one or two, in the afternoon
Sitting down and resting my feet
It didn't take long, conversations begins
Sharing stories and myths
About the world, where we're hurled
A few cheers not to be missed

A few hours later, losing track of the time
Should be getting on my way
Maybe too many, but it's been pretty funny
I can eat again another day
Just one more, before I got to go
I put my bill on the bar
This ones on the house, is the reply
No worries as you have no car

That about settles, to stay a bit longer
Confirmed with another round
Who paid this time, starting to go blind
But smiling at what I found
With only one more to go, what did I know
My glass would always be full
Never to leave, someone said to me
This time it'll never close

Some would get nervous, maybe would bail
But I'm not there quite yet
Feeling to climb, read a few signs
Outside has become all wet
The rain starts to pour, right out the door
Hunkering down from the sight
Play a few tunes, happy as loons
Throughout the endless night

9

Chatter

Hearing all the chatter
From so many flocks that gather
Passing the time
Drinking some wine
Stories on the platter

Flowing to the End

All these bottles, stocked up to drink
I don't care anymore, I don't want to think
Numb the pain of another day
Make it disappear, make it go away
At least for a while, is that too much to ask
If your answer is yes, I'll have another glass
Pour it down, fall on the ground
Only rising, when you hear the sound

Chorus
And it's flowing to the end
No longer any upward trends
Riding down to the sea
On the boat with a friend

With death getting closer, a matter of time
But until then, pour another wine
Or a shot, if it's all you got
Not too picky, a tree with some rot
If you know what I mean, you won't disagree
Having seen too many, of the same old scene
Playing the fool, is all you can do
When all of your troubles, have discovered you

Chorus

Sometimes things work out, others not so much
Can you stand on your own, do you need a crutch
Do you know where you're going, or are you lost
Do you have a purpose, are you with a flock
Seeing the spirals in each and every thing
Nothing you can do, no bells to ring
Just sitting back, have a beer and relax
Down it goes, another glass

Chorus

Gone is the Day

I have to leave
I need to escape
Too many rules
Gone is the day

Have Another Drink

Have another drink, chase away the tears
At the end of another day
No bother to think, only bringing new fears
No longer having much to say
It's all the same, you can win or lose
Nobody knows the end
But until then, living in blues
Listen to the message sent

From so many voices, over the years
Written and on your own
Follow some crumbs, finding a source
Call it a stepping stone
How high you will go, watch out below
Traps are planted everywhere
Falling again, but on a longer trend
None are the worse for wear

Or so you say, but how would you know
All the mirrors you have broke
You could ask a friend, but they're all in a band
Marching where the river flows
Hear the drums of war, the sirens are singing
Calling for you to join
Not this time, preferring some wine
Or with water I'll anoint

One last round, before leaving this town
I've been away too long
Head on home, with this bag of bones
Where you always feel to belong
But where it's found, have looked all around
Never ever found it yet
Until I do, playing the fool
Watch the sun rise and set

In the Afternoon

Taking a break
Having a beer
In the afternoon
Throughout the year

Mid-Afternoon on a Monday

It's mid-afternoon on a Monday
The bar is full, singing is loud
Somebody died on Friday
The ballads are rolling on strong

Another round of shots
No fear left in here
Drown the sorrow see a drop
Down the cheek is a tear

Not lasting long, the singing starts again
It's standing room only
Everyone all drunk, with their friends
Nobody is feeling lonely

It's mid-afternoon on a Monday
The bar is full, singing is loud
Somebody died on Friday
The ballads are rolling on strong

Temps Arising

When the temps arising
You need to get out
Maybe a shower
And sun to dry out

There Are Times

Every once in a while, call it a blue moon
You can feel a smile, hear the calling loon
Where it's from, alive at noon
Enjoy it while it lasts
It won't take long, for a tragic song
In this world, hard to belong
While I'm here, I'll bang the gong
Always over much too fast

Chorus
These are times, with a glass of wine
Embrace the strange, see the signs
It's all the same, the dots and lines
Blurring together, till the end of time

Ringing bells, nobody does come
In this hell, there is no sun
What can you sell, hear the gun
Find yourself in a corner
With nothing to lose, you begin to stand
No more crutches, in a foreign land
See the desert, full of sand
A hermit or a loner

Chorus

Years go by, you can longer count
See the stars, hear the sound
Planting roots, in the ground
Wait for the upcoming rain
Growing fast, up to the sky
No bean stalk, no magic ride
Just a quest, getting high
From the seed in my brain

Chorus

The sun goes down, was it all a dream
Had some fun, wasn't all tragedy
The people I've met, the places I've seen
The only world that I know
Some say others, and I can't disagree
From so long ago, ancient mythology
Riding the boat, in the sky and sea
Into the great unknown

Chorus

Outside

Afternoon Escape

Sitting in the sun, out of the shade
Warming up a sense, enlighten from Hades
Finding your space, away from the pack
An afternoon escape, dreaming is sought

Beer in the Fog

The fog's rolling in, some people call it rain
Haven't seen for so long, the sun winning every day
Others huddled up inside, too cold to let it ride
Not for me, stepping in the outside
I have a full beer, to warm me up
Carry the thoughts, past the broken cup
Feeling the mist, floating around me
Sitting on land, in the drifting sea

Beer in the Garden

Having a beer
In the bar of the garden
Trees, grass, birds and moose
Are the surroundings

Gone Are Reasons

An ale in spring
Wheat in the summer
Wine for the fall
Stout in the winter
All of these brews
A type for the season
No bother what for
Gone are the reasons

Hiding Out

I'll have another drink
To embrace the cold
Getting warmer I think
Start to hear the bold
From dreams of the past
And future yet untold
Forgetting the traps
The young and the old
In between full of trees
The critics take their toll
Open season on the free
Hiding out for home

In the Abyss

In the abyss
Nothing to miss
Seeing the spot
Sparks in the mist

Keeping Warm

The sun warming up
Actions to a frenzy
The sun going down
Flowing drinks aplenty
Keeping warm
A type of energy
Mostly cold
Deep in the sea

Sunny Afternoon

Sitting in the sun
A cold one to slow the think
Eliminate time
With each and every drink

Trees and Streets

Just another pine
In avenues of time
Walking the streets
Feeling the wine

Warming Up

Feel the wind blowing
As sharp as a knife
It is what it is
The storm steals the kite
Getting back inside
Start to warm up
The long winter night
A fire with a cup

Ponderings

A Contemplation

So many times, in the land of the blind
Only the drunk, can see the signs
Of all the games, played every day
Not for the fool, a dragon to slay
Maybe for real or imagination
What's the difference, a contemplation
Who cares in the end, following a trend
Growing the egg, with roots to bend

A Ghost Without a Place

Nobody seems to care when you're at the bottom
Nothing left, no toys to bring, nobody do you follow
Another sad story of losing glory, another tragic scene
It's all the same at the end of day, following the dream

Sometimes you win, mostly lose, empty rooms aplenty
Finding a cave, howl at the moon, nobody looking pretty
Build a fire, walk the wire, make it through to the other side
In the end, begin again, the dot from the black inside

The circles rounding squares, the rules are all broken
Spheres surrounding cubes, the fools pay no token
Shooting up higher, burn off the tires, escape time and space
Landing again, tendencies trend, a ghost without a place

Walk the streets when shadows meet, in the pouring rain
A brand new town bustling around, a million types of games
Hear the tune by the saloon, in an alley to the sky
Playing drunk, a tragic song, a bird losing wings to fly

Afternoon Reflections

Let's finish this beer, and get out of here
Nothing much left, nothing to cheer
Just another day, trying to find a way
A ship at sea, searching for a bay

So many times, we end up alone
All of these places, a temporary home
Change of the scene, look out below
How far will I fall, nobody does know

Find a helping hand, in a foreign land
A life preserver, a crutch to stand
Not every day, but it's nice when we fall
A rope thrown over, the creeping wall

Some people have friends, others have moved on
Finding your place, hearing your song
Sometimes fast and light, others slow and heavy
Damn the torpedoes, a surge on the levy

Walking out the door, escape the madness
Too much chatter, looking for silence
To let things flow, where they're meant to be
Up to the sky, or the bottom of the sea

Bursting the Bubble

Some people settle
On nothing but struggle
Sharing a drink
Bursting the bubble

Crossing the Bridge

I'm sitting here and having a beer
Always open for another cheer
Maybe with others or myself
After a few, will call it lunch
I see you're with friends, don't mind me
A bit too tired, lost at sea
Maybe after we've all had a few rounds
Start to connect, the sights and the sounds
Or if not, another few will do
Whatever it takes, finding the fool
Crossing the bridge, no looking back
Until the morning, wherever we're at

Drunk on the Vine

No more energy
No more time
Having too many
Drunk on the vine

Fill the Broken Cup

Once you've fallen
How do you get up
Forever wondering
Fill the broken cup

Find the Right Pub

So many TVs in every pub you go
Every sports game or news show
All lined up, staring at the screen
Have a drink quick, for the tragic scene

Try to step outside, to clear up your head
Escape distractions, might as well be dead
Lighting up a smoke, and before you know it
Have to put it out, new rules are flowing

Order one more, try to make conversation
Everyone around you, a cell phone direction
Back to your world, a corner in a pub
Slam it down fast, this quest is done

Cutting your losses, moving onto another
Just like before, no need to enter
Walk around an hour, without a welcome sign
Just then I see, one that might be fine

Walking on in, it looks a thousand years old
In the middle a tree, surrounded by stools
Guitars and drums, every beer to imagine
An old man walking in, grinning like the comic

After an hour, the pics were smoking
Feeling the beat, the drums are pounding
Smiles everywhere, we're all in the band
Playing until we can no longer stand

From Each Day

Feel the pain
From each day
That you're born
Or fade away

Hassles

The social police
Are moving in
Can no longer drink
Over the railing

I Can Barely Stand

The problem with drinking is losing the thinking
No longer aware of the audience
And what you find funny, is dreaming of money
All of the choices and wants
So what do you do, when falling to fool
With all of the jokes set up
Let the punch lines ring, a smile to bring
If not, fill another cup

Chorus
All I'd like to do is sit back and relax
Maybe if lucky have a few laughs
If you think I'm getting out of hand
Not to worry, I can barely stand

Speak too loud, from too many rounds
Landing on a reaching ear
It could be funny, or even some envy
Laughing at another's fears
Otherwise confusion, will not be amusing
The joke lost in the wind
Thinking it's about them, the ongoing trend
Might as well throw it in the bin

Chorus

It might seem all wrong, going too strong
But you have to understand
To find the dreams, from a different scene
Have to lose all your hands
While certainly not needed, it's an ancient healing
Call it a crutch if you will
I'll have another please, maybe some mead
Or a week old glass of swill

Chorus

I'm Still Here

Sitting in the bar, in the afternoon
I'm not the only one, who saw too much too soon
Getting through the day, get ready for the night
How I ended up this way, a roll of the dice

Chorus
But I'm here, I'm still here
I'll have a glass of beer
I won't shed a tear
Until I'm gone

An hour starts rolling by, nobody stops to say hi
I finish the beer and step outside
Go for a walk, a whopping ten steps
Into another, a trapeze act

Chorus

Have another round, start flowing down
If I have too many, I'm on the ground
Where did I end up, can't recognize the scene
Is it reality, or just another dream

Chorus

Lost in Hades

Where is my
Ship of Jays
Did it get lost
In the maze of Hades

Message Intentions

What is the message
What did you hear
Who was the sender
A purpose to clear

So many around you
There is no doubt
Learning the language
The signs screaming out

What to do with messages sent
For the dogs who guard the bridge
The nine rings to the bottom
The seven steps up the ridge

A haven or a warning
Sometimes hard to tell
The message is a yearning
Another way to sell

An idea or dream to focus
All your energies
Choices of directions
Only one that you need

Messy Hair

My hair is all messy
But I don't really care
Receive everything
Into the lair
Maybe one day I'll cut it
A comb to straighten out
But until then the seeds
Seem right to sprout

Might As Well Stay Home

I was talking to a bloke
And he told me his complaint
Can no longer drink with a smoke
In any public place or joint
It seemed pretty absurd
No longer inside or the cold
Seeming just a matter of time
Before they all up and fold
Such a tragic scene
Blocking all the roads
Never getting it together
Might as well stay home

Mirrors Are Sent

All your wants and choices
They're yours to the end
Swimming in your drivel
Mirrors will be sent

No More Places

There's no more places
For people that dream
The tragedy shown
Flowing down the stream

Nobody is Having Fun

Nobody is having fun
Nobody is having fun
Too many rules in the sun
Nobody is having fun

Shadows That Pass

The water is rising
How long will it last
In the end is only
Shadows that pass

Silence in Charge

Some people are shy
To protect insecurities
Other are dry
To prevent hostilities
Either or
Silence in charge
Seeing the dream
Escaping the yard

Silent to Know

Sitting alone
A home for the stranger
Grabbing a throne
A chair in the corner

Hearing of travels
From others gone by
His own is kept
Somewhere inside

Some have dreams
Of places to go
Others are keen
Silent to know

The Home Brewer

If I had a place, somewhere in the hills
I'd build a barn, for barrels and stills
All sorts of beers, brewed for a try
Plenty of mead, honey won't die
The whites and reds, brandy and ports
Whiskey and vodka, for winters in shorts
Rum and tequila, for hot summer weather
At least a few more, ingredients to wander
I'm sure there'd be problems, with brewing so many
Too much tasting, explosions fermenting
With years going by, the barn is bulging with booze
Time for a party and try out the new
Try to invite others, but living so remote
Only fur and feathers, see the welcome note
No big deal, they like the meal and stay
After a year, they're settled and say
Thanks for drinks, but we've had some time to think
We know of many more, ingredients for your drink
What happens next, the plants and roots fall in
They completely take over, smiling with a grin
After a week they say it's ready, handing me a cup
Cheering with a thanks, pouring bottoms up
Getting tired and weary, laying down to sleep
Dreaming in a hurry, no fog is left to creep
Waking up refreshed, no signs of hung over
Life continued on, with only one brew to order
Only need a drop, for each pint that is poured
Any more and you'll be, human no more

Tragic Ending

I'm so alone, there's nothing I can do
Any friends I meet, melt away too soon
Any home I find, a temporary stay
Looking out for doors, blind for the day

Chorus
It's always a tragic ending, any hope that you feel
Learning from the mending, walking the unreal
Have another shot, have another beer
Drown out the past, burn up the fears

We all must go on, directions in the road
Some are never ending detours, the choices that we know
Reach a new peak, seeing where you fell
How much further you need to go, escape from the well

Chorus

Evenings

A Lone Whistle Blowing

Hear the pipes maintaining
The sound of the song
A lone whistle blowing
Humming where we belong

After a Long Day

Walking into the pub, after such a long day
Feels like been up, for a couple days straight
Sitting down at the stool, order a brew
Drink it up quick, seeking the fool

Order up a second, see what the juke box offers
Would prefer a house guitar, no point to argue
Add a dozen songs, to chill for an hour
Back to the bar, ready for another

Order up a third, let's have a conversation
Feeling a bit lively, here for the duration
Talk about what's wrong, vent a little bit
A joke and a song, laughing how it is

Order up a fourth, stepping out for some air
Watch the setting sun, on the horizon clear
See the birds flying, back to their nests
Probably do the same, in a few minutes

Order up a fifth, this will be the last
Not much longer, before I'll crash
As I pour back the glass, fall on the floor
Standing up again and out the door

Bounty for All

Hear the music playing, a dozen strings or more
Feel the spirit rising, a natural place to soar
With no words to describe, the highs and the lows
A bounty for all, where the tunes will flow

Don't Close the Bar

The rain is flooding
What do you do
Don't close the bar

Drunken Dreams

Walking down a street, sun going down
Curious feet, a brand new town
On the shore
The lights go on, the music plays
A mystic song, for the ship of jays
Having just arrived before
I walked in, scanned the scene
Tried to think, is this a dream
From days of yore
Sat at the bar, had the house special
A pint of lager, a couple of pretzels
Find out what's in store

It might be the same, or a bit different
Nobody to blame, for the moment
That you're in
Hear the beats of the drums, the piano play
The guitar being strummed, the flute to raise
Your eyes again
To catch the show, so loud and clear
Brought in the boat, that never fears
The end
Where it starts, to celebrate
A brand new part, call it a new day
To begin

But that's a little later, a neighbor said
See if you can make it, through the dread
Until morning
It's not so bad, it could be worse
Seven nights had, left a curse
I'm still learning
It won't be long, before the dragons come
You'll hear a gong, as the moon
Is rising
My advice to you, get out quick
Or play the fool, always tricks
Are deceiving

I turn around, looking outside
On the ground, are fire eyes
And staring
Right at me, I fall back
I couldn't believe, where my current track
Is heading
It's no worry, they can't come in
A home for the weary, a shot of gin
For seeing
Here's what we'll do, a game of cards
For the one that loses, in the yard
For feeding

This is a joke, scanning everyone
I'm the last bloke, before the setting sun
That walked in the door
The first shall be last, the last shall be first
But you get a chance, delay the worst
If a low card is yours
The cards are dealt, everyone looks around
Who will start, fate is found
Rolling over
I flip mine up, an ace of spades
Empty the cup, down to Hades
Falling on the floor

I get pulled up to stand, a spear is thrust,
In my hand, do what you must,
Good luck
Out the door I went, walked or pushed,
I have to admit, my thirst was quenched,
Felt as strong as an ox
I looked around, as the dragons near,
Down to the ground, a hole is clear,
Just like the fox
Down I go, about a hundred feet,
The dragons know, where to meet,
When flying out of the box

To a hole in the cliffs, along the shore
At least fifty feet, above the floor
I'm reaching
Down through the air, landing on the back
Of a dragon that dared, to change the track
I'm heading
I told him no more, laughed at the games
A secret lore, going down in flames
I'm tending
Didn't take long, back to the pub
Hearing the song, pouring jugs
I'm landing

Walking back in, all the heads turn
Who's next to begin, feel the burn
I'm done
Have another glass, you made it through
Seemed pretty fast, what did you do
It appears that you won
After a few drinks, crash to the floor
Wake up and blink, on different shore
In the sun
Was is it all dream, surrounded by today
The modern scene, a dock on a bay
The end of another run

Fading Out and In

Listen to the music, streaming from your head
In between the blinks, when going to bed
The highs and lows, fading and slow
Until the dream, showing to know
From where or why, one at a time
Seeing the symbols, a language of signs
Follow along, a hill or a lake
Riding the air, feeling to wake

I Feel Blue

I feel blue, so blue
There's nothing more that I can do
The sun is setting too
I feel blue

Late Summer Moments

Sitting in the sun
Dripping down sweat
Having a beer
The sun about to set

Laying Down

Laying down
With dreams ahead
From the past
A cast of dread

Of the future
A stranger scene
So confused
What does it mean

Float in a whirlpool
Round and down
See the sirens
Wanting known

All your fears
Gone in a flash
No need for things
Time or cash

Music Streams

Of all the types of music
That I've heard in my life
None will carry me further
Then the drums, strings and pipes
Playing together
An ever winding stream
Until the fall
Losing the dream

Not a Moment Too Soon

Who knows why or what for
We're here at all, primitive lore
Who really cares with bills to pay
Spinning the wheels, day after day

Going faster and faster, becoming a blur
The world getting smaller, ending the curls
No more spirals, no more dreams
All are tired, the same old scene

Have a drink, play a tune, time to wake up
Smash it all if you have a full cup
Feel the beats, the strings and the flute
Alive again, not a moment too soon

Starting the Song

Hear the music playing
Connecting to the dream
The dragons left for burning
Changing of the scene
Why or how the ruse
The tree is gone
Made into guitars and flutes
Starting up the song

Too Much

I can no longer stand
Don't bother to help
I'll fall on the land
Some ring a bell
No longer caring
Looking towards the sky
The world is spinning
Or am I inside

Waking Up the Dream

Hearing strings for dancing
A hum settles in
Up and down are prancing
No care for the rain
The playing never stops
Waking up the dream
The ever growing crop
Music fills the streams

Jokers

Comic is Missed

Some people settle
For wants of bliss
Float in the kettle
The comic is missed

Forever the Comic

It may seem tragic
It may seem blue
Forever the comic
Laughing in the noose

Freeing the Fool

Some people say, I drink too much
Seeing them standing with their crutch
Tragic it may be, going down in the scene
In the end will be laughing, the fool was set free

Joker in Command

Who controls who, the left or the right
Since the dawn of time, the day or night
Seeing the cycles, of repetitive plans
Watching the joker, always in command
Born into tragic, never escape the fall
Evolve the comic, climbing the wall
With laughter ever after, where the boat goes
Else on a river, to the ocean it flows

Jokes to Trade

It used to be tragic
The loss that was made
Evolving the comic
With jokes left to trade

Laughing Inside

How to survive
In a world full of lies
Finding the fool
Laughing inside

Laughing Not to Miss

For all the mistakes I've made
For all the times I've not seen
For all the lines in the shade
For all the signs ignored complete

I can't go back, only forward
The ships are leaving port
Where they land, we're all a steward
Keeping open or a fort

How to find the magic line
Riding off the edge of a cliff
Have a beer or glass of wine
Laughing not to miss

Laughing Upside Down

For all the pubs that banned me
For jokes that went too far
A little harsh I think you'd agree
Escaping from the yard
Maybe one day, you'll find yourself
A stranger in the town
No longer knowing the rules to play
Laughing upside down

Nobody Knows

As the bars start to close
Where can one go
To relax with a few
Nobody knows

Only the Roots

When shadows fall
In gardens of plenty
Only the roots
Remain being funny

Shooting Pool

Shooting pool
The clown and the fool
Down the hole
A dream is through

Somebody Sneezed

Starting so small, left all alone
Before you know it, out of control
How did it happen, who was in charge
It's nobody's fault, just stacking the cards
One after another, how was I to know
That it became reality, watching the show
Where did it come from, how did it get so big
Who know or cares anymore, it is what is
As the years rolled along, built up some speed
Reaching the clouds, higher than trees
What happened next, you know how it ends
Somebody sneezed, dust in the wind

Staying Up Late

Staying up late, to the dawn of the day
Owls all night, in the morning a Jay
How it happened, one after another
So many steps, others don't bother
Friend to the turtle, the mule and the wolf
Through hills and valleys, follow a brook
Leaving the thief, in trees collecting
Seeking the joker, when lost in direction

The Clown or the Fool

We're all alone
There nothing we can do
Except the part
Play the clown or fool

The Dream Master

When dealing with trust
One is often thrust
Into the fire
From all the liars
With the only escape
Start to betray
Promises made
Never to stay
The only thing lasting
Grows from the fasting
Surging with dreams
Merging the scenes
Following faster
End with the master
That makes up the rules
Defined as the fool

Trend From a Trait

There is an answer
There is a fate
A joke to deliver
A trend from a trait

Cheers

Cheers to Chances

We have so many troubles
We have so many fears
All are gone in a flash
With another cheer
The past mistakes
Lessons were learned
In the end, a quest
Another chance, for the burn

Cheers to the Seasons

When it's cold
A pint of Guinness
When it's warm
A bit of sweetness
Sometimes wine
With a meal
A shot to climb
Where cowards kneel
All these drinks
And so many more
Finding dreams
With every pour

Drinks

Have a drink
Have a cheer
Drown the sorrows
Lose the fear

Give Me Something Strong

Give me something strong
It's freezing cold outside
Melt the ice, bang the gong
Warming up inside
Will sing an old time song
Dancing all night long
Against the wind, a rising tide
Give me something strong

Good Luck

All the wants and the choices
A downward spiral that will last
Good luck to one and all
That find themselves on the path

Have Another Drink For Me

Have another drink for me
I wish I could stay but gotta go
On another ship but I remember thee
And the times we did know
Maybe make it two or three
Been so long, lost at sea
Who knows when, we'll see again
Have another drink for me

Here's To

Here's to the rebels, that died at the end
Here's to the struggles, and all of our friends
Here's to the fight, in finding the truth
Here's to the right, crossing the sleuth

Here's to the painter, capture the moment
Here's to the writer, escaping the torment
Here's to musicians, striking a chord
Here's to intuition, showing there's more

Here's to the lessons, never again
Here's to confession, healing begins
Here's to the dream, that hasn't yet died
Here's to the scene, visions inside

Here's to the start, of another new day
Here's to the end, of repetitive ways
Here's to the fall, of houses of cards
Here's to the rise, beating the odds

Home Brew

I'll take a fresh brewed home brew
Over a brand any time
Pouring down what I know is true
Some beer, mead or wine
Knowing where it comes from
Seeing all the signs
Always having more fun
Growing my own vines

How About That First Drink

How about that first drink
To start us on our way
No longer any time to think
Been doing that all day
And after that one more
To open up new doors
Where it goes, we never know
How about that first drink

Late Night Cheer

Here's to ignorance is bliss
Or the tragedy of reality
Forever escaping to comedy

Making It Through

Fill up the glass
At least one or two
For all of our struggles
And making it through

Maybe Just One More Drink

Maybe just one more drink
Before I really gotta go
I know I've been saying so long
But this time you outta know
I have lots of things to do
I really should be moving on
But I'm having such a good time
Maybe just one more drink

Over the Years

Relax with a beer
Losing the fear
Drying the tears
Over the years

Past the Brink

Numb the pain, drown the tears
Feel the silence, sorrow and fears
Another drink, to ride the edge
Past the brink, beyond the dead

Seeing the Beauty in Everything

Seeing the beauty in everything
Hearing the songs that others sing
The paths that we all, struggle to tread
Before the time, we go to bed
Before the bells, start to ring
Having a laugh, from meandering
Moving up, beyond the dread
Seeing the beauty in everything

Strangers

I am a stranger
And so are all of you
Stuck on this land
Full of thieves and fools

Throwing Logs

Have some wine, have some bread
Left and right, full of dread
Follow dots, light and dark
Seeing spots, another spark
Throwing logs, get it raging high
Even the rain, cannot deny
Just the way it goes, all must end
In order to be, born again

Time To Be Going

Only a few hours left of this wonderful trip
Before it's time to be going
Had such a great time, drank bottles of wine
The spirits were ever flowing

To Fools and Jokers

Here's to the ones that discover the core
Here's to the fools, that fall on the floor
Here's the jokers, whose lines are misplaced
Here's to the end, of another long day